Acknowledgments

Every day of my life begins with thinking of my mother and thanking her in gratitude for all she has done for us. I'm not sure if I will ever be able to repay her for the selfless care and unconditional love that she showered upon us. My mother quietly worked to give us a better life, never once complaining or reminding us of things she did for us.

I know what true love is because of her. And to know love is to know God. I wish I could see her one more time and tell her how lucky I was to have her as my mother. Oh, my mother, how I miss her very much. I know in my heart I will meet her one day, and when that time comes, I want to make sure she is proud of me.

I also want to thank my father, who is the best role model I could ask for. He was a very kind, humble human being. For him, actions always spoke louder than words.

And of course, I want to thank my brothers and sister, who have helped me throughout my life. Their genuine love and affection have been a strong pillar of support in my life.

My wife (Areeba) has been great. She has continued to support me, no matter what, and has allowed me to focus on things that I love such as teaching squash and writing.

The list of friends that have helped me is super long. I won't be able to include everyone's name here, but still: Jim Rutherford, Natalie Ali Khan, Viq Anwar, Vikrant Gandhi, Hamza Ahmed, Shahzad Ahmad, Fadoua Zemmouri, Dr. Hamed Ghazali, Manal Kazia, and Majid Zamman have been extremely supportive of my efforts in writing this book.

Special thanks to Aries Jones, Mike Vance, and Marla Garcia from Night Heron Media and Mike Guillory from Mike Guillory Design & Illustration for their help with editing, illustrating and publishing this book. It has been really great working with you.

Finally, I want to thank my daughters, Rania and Halima, who make me smile and proud every day. They have filled my life with more love than I could ever imagine. It is a special blessing to have them in my life. I always look forward to the mornings when I wake them, and spend more time with them every evening before bed. I love them not with my heart or mind; the heart can stop and the mind can forget, and so I love them with my soul.

أَعُوذُ وَا بِاللَّهِ مِنَ الشَّيْطَانِ الرَّجِيمِ

بِسْمِ اللَّهِ الرَّحْمَنِ الرَّحِيمِ

Fatima woke up early one Sunday morning to get ready for online Quran Sunday School.

First, she brushed her teeth, made her bed, then ate her favorite breakfast downstairs with her sister, Noor, and her Mama.

After breakfast, Fatima went to the living room and opened up her Mama's laptop to start her class. At 10 am, her Sunday School teacher, Mrs. Salma Khan, appeared on the screen and greeted her and the rest of the students. Then, everyone talked about their week at school and plans for the weekend. But, it wasn't long until Mrs. Salma Khan began to lead the class into the lesson for the day. "Please open up your Quran to Chapter 51, Adh-Dhariyat, 'The Winnowing Winds,'" she said nicely.

The Pillars of Islam:

Shahada (Faith)
Salah (Prayer)
Sawm (Fasting)
Zakat (Almsgiving)
Hajj (Pilgrimage)

Belief in Islam is to believe in Allah, His Angels, His Books, His Apostles, the meeting with Him, and to believe in the Resurrection.

FATIMA RECEIVES ALLAH'S LOVE

All of the students, including Fatima, attentively listened to Mrs. Salma Khan, taking notes as she spoke and raising their hands for questions when they had them.

Before Fatima realized it, the class was almost over! "Now, I would like to end the class with an Aya for you all to think about for next week's class," Mrs. Salma Khan said. From the chapter they were working on, she recited:

Sūrat Adh-Dhāriyāt (Winnowing Winds)

– *Wama khalaqtu aljinna waal-insa illa liyaAAbudooni.*

"That Allah put Human and Jinn on this planet to worship him."

O Allah, help me remember you, be grateful to you, and worship you in an excellent manner.

FATIMA RECEIVES ALLAH'S LOVE

7

Right after Mrs. Salma Khan said the verse, Fatima became confused. She had no idea what the Aya meant! "Mrs. Salma Khan," she asked politely, "I don't get what that Aya means. Could you please explain it to me?"

"Oh, I'm so sorry, Fatima," Mrs. Salma Khan replied, "Class is over, and there's not enough time for me to review this Aya. We can certainly talk about it more during next week's class."

"Oh...that's okay. Thank you, Mrs. Salma Khan," Fatima said quietly. But everything was not okay. Fatima really wanted to know what it meant, and she didn't know if she could wait a whole week!

O My Lord! Increase me in knowledge.

FATIMA RECEIVES ALLAH'S LOVE

9

While Mama was preparing her and her sister's, Noor's, lunch, Fatima sat at the dining table deep in thought.

What did that Aya mean. Does it mean we should pray all the time and recite the Quran or Zikr and fast? What if there's not enough time to do all of that? How do I find the time to go to school, and do my homework, and learn piano, and make art, and play squash, and eat at restaurants and get our favorite ice cream, and sleep, and…

Part of being a good Muslim is leaving away that which does not concern him.

FATIMA RECEIVES ALLAH'S LOVE

"Fatima!" Her Mama exclaimed, pulling her out of her thoughts. "Are you okay? You've been sitting at the table so quietly. Why aren't you playing with your sister like you usually do every weekend?"

"Mama," Fatima said sadly, with tears forming in her eyes, "I don't want to make Allah angry with me…"

"Oh, Fatima, what do you mean? What happened with Sunday School?" Then, Fatima told her mom everything, including the new Aya she learned and how she didn't want to wait for Mrs. Salma Khan to explain it next week, and why she was worried about making Allah upset.

"I don't want to make Allah angry by being disobedient. I want to worship all the time, but how do I do that and do everything I love doing, like playing with Noor? It's impossible!" Fatima said, throwing her hands into the air and putting her head down on the table.

The best of you in Islam is the best of you in character when you possess understanding.

FATIMA RECEIVES ALLAH'S LOVE

Mama laughed. "Oh, dear Fatima, yes, it's true that Allah put Human and Jinn on the planet to worship him, but that doesn't mean what you think."

"Really?" Fatima said quietly, lifting her head back up.

"Really! What that Aya means is as long as we always remember our Creator, and remember to do it for His sake, and follow our beloved Prophet Muhammad, peace be upon him, whatever we do day and night, we will become closer to Him, and He will love us in return."

A light sparkled in Fatima's eye. "So, does that mean I can still play with Noor, go to school, eat my favorite food, and sleep and still pray to Allah Subhanaho Wa Taala?"

"Of course you can! It is very easy. How about this—I'll write down a list of things you and your sister should remember to do each day that makes Allah happy so you always receive His love." Mama then got up from the table and eventually returned with the notebook and a pencil, and scribbled a to-do list for Fatima:

The best of charity is when a Muslim man gains knowledge, then teaches it to his Muslim brother.

How to Receive

Be Kind
Be kind to your friends, teachers, and everyone and everything you meet, including animals and plants.

Seek Knowledge
Gain knowledge so you can use it to help others when you grow up.

Perform Good Deeds
Small actions like picking up trash or giving to charity make a big difference in our world.

Allah's Love

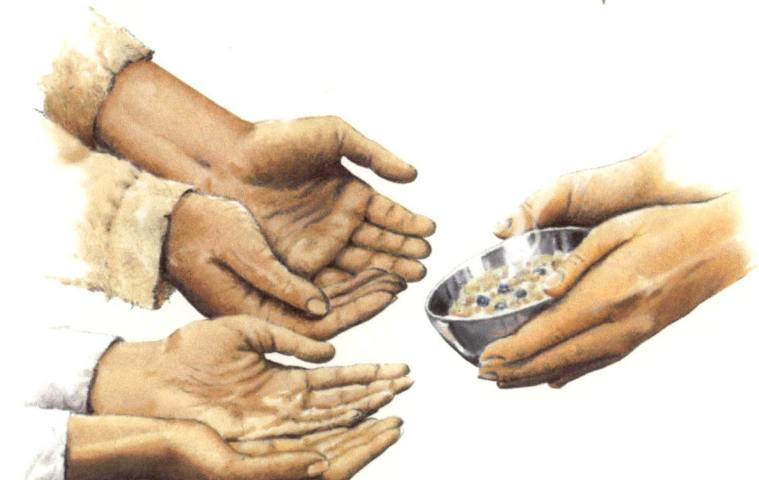

Care for Others
Put others before yourself. Our religion, Islam, teaches us to put others' happiness before our own to achieve peace. If you make others happy, then you will always be happy as well.

Keep Everything Clean
Keep everything nice and clean, from our home to the community. As the Prophet, Muhammad, PBUH said:

(Cleanliness is half the faith.)

Stay Healthy and Strong

Every good thing you do for others will start with you, and that requires you to be strong. As Prophet Muhammad said:

(A strong believer is better and dearer to Allah than a weak one, and both are good.) Exercise and eating good food are very important to keep yourself healthy.

Always Love and Respect Yourself

As you respect others and offer love, remember to do the same for yourself. Remember who you are, and always be proud of yourself, from how you look to your religion and culture.

Pray Before Bedtime

You can do this by thinking about how grateful you are to Allah for everything He has provided us so we can live a very happy life.

GOOD!

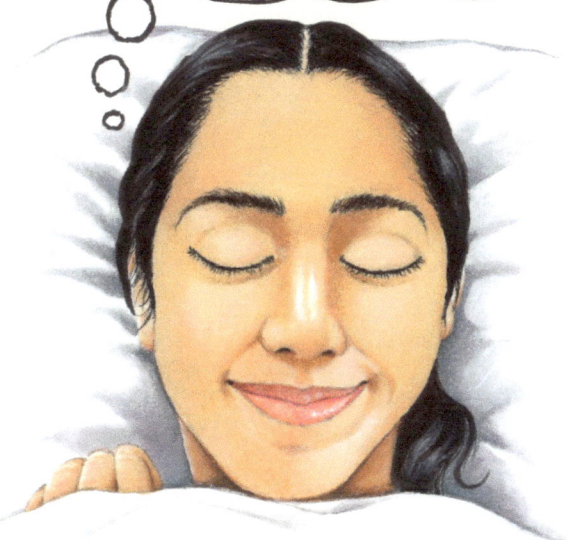

Stay Positive

Keep an attitude of gratitude, no matter what kind of challenges you face. As you lay in bed at night, also think about all the good things you can do for others once you wake up in the morning. When you grow up, think about how you will serve the world.
And always say, "Alhamdulillah."

Do Everything with Good Intentions

Our Prophet Muhammad, PBUH said:

(Actions are according to intentions, and everyone will get what he or she intended.) Having an intention for every physical act that we do is very important; it helps us have purpose.

Fatima read Mama's list and smiled. "Thank you, Mama. I'll make sure to hang this up in our room so we can follow this every single day...starting now!" She jumped up from the table and gave her mom the biggest hug she could muster. "Can I share this list with my Quran class next week, too?"

"Of course you can, Fatima!" Mama said grinning back at Fatima. Then, Fatima ran from the table and up the stairs to go find Noor so they could begin working on Mama's list together.

Throughout the day, the girls shared their toys with one another, read their favorite books, and helped Mama clean around the house.

They went through their closet and set aside all the clothes they no longer wore so they could donate them to charity.

Verily, the most complete of believers in faith are those with the best character and who are most kind to their families.

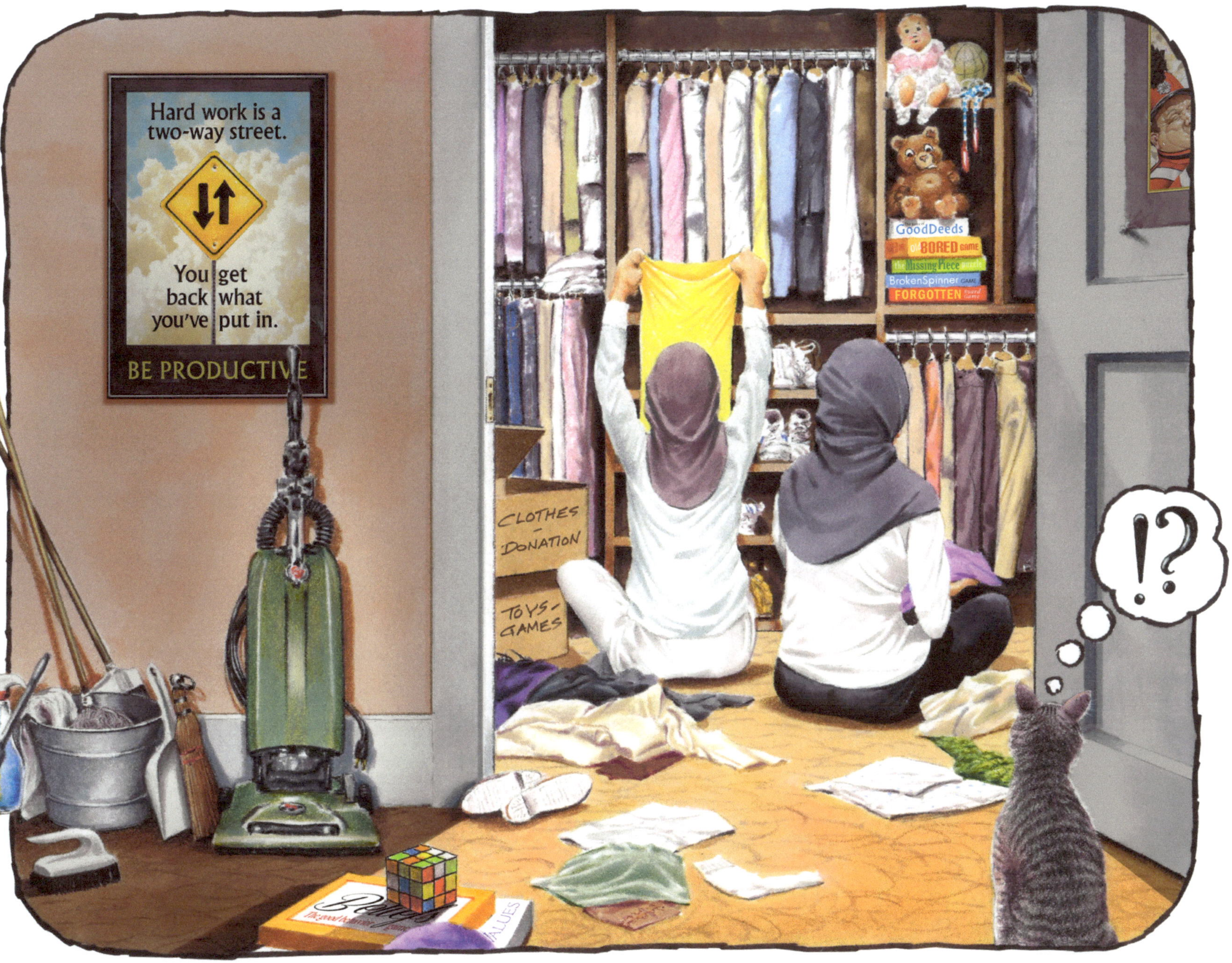
Hard work is a two-way street.
You get back what you've put in.
BE PRODUCTIVE
GoodDeeds
BORED
Missing Piece
BrokenSpinner
FORGOTTEN
CLOTHES - DONATION
TOYS-GAMES
!?

When it was time for dinner, they ate all of their vegetables, even the greenest ones!

Soon, it was time for bed, and Fatima and Noor were so happy they were able to check off every single thing from the list...almost!

That night, the girls laid in their beds, looking up at the ceiling. Fatima closed her eyes and started praying from the heart.

Thank you for everything you've provided us, Allah, so me and my sister and my Mama and everyone on the earth can live a happy, peaceful life. When I grow up, I will become a doctor so I can help children, animals, or anyone else who needs help throughout my life. Inshallah.

Fatima reached over to her bed stand and crossed the last three things on the list before turning off her light. Soon after, she fell asleep, with a soft smile on her face.

Glory is to Allah, and praise is to Him— by the multitude of his creation, by His pleasure, by the weight of His throne, and by the extent of His words.

In the middle of the night, Fatima found herself in a dream. She was still in her and her sister's room, but it was dark, with the moonlight shining through their window. Everything looked the same, except for a figure that was now seated in the corner. It was an old man who was writing inside of a big book placed on top of his lap.

Fatima sat up from her bed quickly. At first, she was scared. Who was this old man? What was he doing in her and her sister's room? But then he looked up from his book, met Fatima's eyes, and spoke.

"Hi, Fatima. I am an angel. It's very nice to meet you."

"Hi—hi, Angel. What are you doing here?" Fatima was still anxious. She had never seen an angel before.

"I'm here to write down the names of who Allah Subhanaho Wa Taala loves."

"Oh." Fatima relaxed a little bit, but was nervous about her next question. "Are our names in the book?"

"Hmm. Let's see here…" The angel muttered, adjusting the spectacles on his face.

O Allah forgive me, have mercy on me, guide me, support me, protect me, provide for me, and elevate me.

FATIMA RECEIVES ALLAH'S LOVE

25

Minutes passed, but to Fatima, it seemed like forever since the angel had started looking for her and her sister's name. *Maybe he needs help looking for us on such a big list,* she thought to herself, which was followed by another, more worrisome thought: *or maybe we're not in the book at all…*

Suddenly feeling frantic, Fatima hopped out of bed and ran over to the angel's side. "Please tell me our names are there, Angel! They have to be!" Her eyes began to water.

"My Lord, I am in need of whatever good you send down to me."

FATIMA RECEIVES ALLAH'S LOVE

"Ah..." The Angel removed his spectacles and looked at Fatima with softened eyes. "Well, take a look for yourself," he said, as he turned the open book toward Fatima to read.

Shaking, Fatima took the book from the Angel's hands, and upon reading, her tears began to dry. She was relieved and very happy to see that at the very top of the list, were her and her sister's names, written in beautiful gold ink.

Our Lord! We believe; then do Thou forgive us and have mercy upon us—for Thou art the best of those who show mercy.

FATIMA RECEIVES ALLAH'S LOVE

The next morning, Fatima woke up, happier than ever, and immediately ran downstairs to tell Mama and Baba about the great dream she had.

"See?" Mama then said with a smile. "Stick to that list of faith, and you'll find that you'll always receive Allah's love."

Inshaa Allah.

FATIMA RECEIVES ALLAH'S LOVE

NIGHT HERON MEDIA

PO Box 5872
Katy, Texas 77491

Copyright © 2023 Muhammad Sadiq
No part of this book may be reproduced in any form or by any electronic or mechanical means, including information storage and retrieval devices or systems, without prior written permission from the publisher, except that brief passages may be quoted for reviews.

ISBN: 979-8-218-17819-2

10   9   8   7   6   5   4   3   2   1

Library of Congress Cataloging-in-Publication Data on file with the publisher.

Editors: Aries Jones, Mike Vance
Designer & Illustrator: Mike Guillory

www.ingramcontent.com/pod-product-compliance
Lightning Source LLC
LaVergne TN
LVHW072306070526
838201LV00100B/288